T0156905

TRY ME, I AM JESUS.

*A Muslim's Journey
with Christ*

SYED IBN SYED

Copyright © 2015 Syed Ibn Syed.

All rights reserved. No part of this book may be used or reproduced by any means, graphic, electronic, or mechanical, including photocopying, recording, taping or by any information storage retrieval system without the written permission of the publisher except in the case of brief quotations embodied in critical articles and reviews.

WestBow Press books may be ordered through booksellers or by contacting:

WestBow Press
A Division of Thomas Nelson & Zondervan
1663 Liberty Drive
Bloomington, IN 47403
www.westbowpress.com
1 (866) 928-1240

Because of the dynamic nature of the Internet, any web addresses or links contained in this book may have changed since publication and may no longer be valid. The views expressed in this work are solely those of the author and do not necessarily reflect the views of the publisher, and the publisher hereby disclaims any responsibility for them.

All Scripture quotations are from *The NIV Study Bible (NIV)* Copyright © 1985 by The Zondervan Corporation. All rights reserved

All Quranic references are from, *The Holy Qurán with Full Arabic Text, English Translation* by Abdullah Yusuf Ali, by Dar Al-Furqan, Beirut, Lebanon

All the Hadith quotations are from *Sahih Bukhari*, Translated by M. Muhsin Khan, 1st edition Edited by: Mika'il al-Almany Created: 2009-10-02 17:41:54 Last modified: 2009-10-11 23:46:24 Version: 0910112346244624-2

Any people depicted in stock imagery provided by Thinkstock are models, and such images are being used for illustrative purposes only. Certain stock imagery © Thinkstock.

ISBN: 978-1-4908-8339-7 (sc)
ISBN: 978-1-4908-8338-0 (e)

Library of Congress Control Number: 2015908813

Print information available on the last page.

WestBow Press rev. date: 6/22/2015

WESTBOW*
P R E S S
A DIVISION OF THOMAS NELSON
& ZONDERVAN

Contents

Jesus answered, *"Everyone who drinks this water (from the well) will be thirsty again, but whoever drinks the water I give him will never thirst. Indeed, the water I give him will become in him a spring of water welling up to eternal life."* —John 4:13–14

To my beloved wife, Grace,

a faithful partner, a wise counselor, and a never-failing friend.

ACKNOWLEDGEMENTS

To thank all the people who have helped make this book a reality would require tens of pages just to mention their names. Nevertheless, I would like to express my heartfelt gratitude to certain individuals who have contributed toward this book.

I would like to thank my family, without whom this venture would have been utterly impossible. My wife and my children have been extremely supportive of me in writing this book, graciously sacrificing many of our family hours. My wife has been a constant source of encouragement during the times when I hesitated for my story to be made public.

I would like to thank our friend Anna for reading and editing the manuscript numerous times and for being patient with me and all my grammatical errors as she helped refine my English. Thanks also to Mark, our dear friend and brother, who made many helpful suggestions to make the book more reader friendly. Our thanks go as well to Brad and Al, friends who have helped with publicizing the book.

Thanks to my dear friend, Stephen, for his designing expertise in the cover design and layout of the book.

My thanks go to all our team members for your encouragement and for bearing with me when I went on and on about the project.

Thanks to my publisher, WestBowPress, for encouraging me during the final stages of publication.

Thanks to the countless people who have contributed financially and helped in so many invaluable ways.

Most of all I give thanks to my Lord and Savior, Jesus Christ, without whom I would not have even existed in the first place nor had this story to tell.

ABOUT *the* AUTHOR

Syed Ibn Syed was on the verge of suicide when the miraculous happened, and he gave his life to Jesus instead. A former Muslim, he has been walking with Christ for a quarter of a century and maintains a deep passion and love for Muslim people. Because of his background, Syed is equipped to share the gospel and the love of Jesus in unique ways. He has a master's degree in religion, speaks nine different languages, and conducts seminars and conferences in various countries. This book is not only an account of his incredible journey with Christ but also a celebration of the love and grace of God.

Introduction

When friends began encouraging me to write the story of my journey with Christ, I was not entirely convinced people would want to hear what I had to say. However, over the years, as many expressed how the Lord had blessed and encouraged them through my testimony, I was compelled to record my story so that others might read and profit from it.

It is a privilege to share my story in the hope that all who read it, be they Christian, Muslim, or otherwise, will witness the wonder of God working in the lives of His people. I have attempted to present certain gospel terms in a manner that is easily understood. It has not been my intention to hurt the religious sentiments of anyone, especially Muslims. My desire is that Muslims will read my story without bias and see the love of Christ through this book. May the Lord bless you and speak to you as you read.

"In the Beginning"

Genesis 1:1

It was nearly nine o'clock on the night of December 24, 1990. I was seventeen years old, sitting alone in a park, contemplating the recent turn of events. My mind was racing back and forth between incidents that could potentially have a very debilitating effect on my entire family. Wave after wave of emotions crashed through my soul. I was feeling angry, upset, sad, and lost. Yes, that was the word, lost. I had no one to turn to for help. The future seemed so bleak, and the more I thought about it, the more it seemed to be slipping away into oblivion. Everything was so confusing; a host of questions bombarded my mind. Why were things happening the way they were? Ours was a very good, God-fearing family. Then why these problems? Was Allah not pleased with me? Had I failed in any of my duties toward Allah? I had tried to keep my eyes and thoughts focused on the Almighty and had striven to fulfill the requirements of Islam to the best of my knowledge. Then why had this storm brewed in my family? I cried out toward Allah, the Almighty, Most Beneficent, and Merciful, yet the heavens seemed strangely distant. As I sat deep in thought, one question superseded all others. What use is this life after all that has happened?

My father raised us in accordance with all that the Islamic faith demands. He was and still is a devout Muslim. I remember him teaching my sister and me the importance and the honor of being a Muslim. He often said, "Islam is the best religion in the world" or "All other religions are only secondary to Islam." At home and in the mosque, this idea was taught, preached, and firmly embedded in the mind and the heart of every Muslim.

I took great pleasure in performing all the duties of Islam. My chest would puff up with pride every time I said, "I am a Muslim."

The Imam would say, "Islam is the ultimate goal of a human's search for God. Nothing in the world can satisfy a human heart other than the five daily prayers of Islam."

He also said, "Once your good deeds surpass your bad ones, if Allah wills, He shall give you a place in paradise." I desired to gain the favor of Allah by doing all that was prescribed in Islam.

My family was a traditional Sunni Islamic family, so my parents brought me up in a strict Islamic environment. My younger sister and I used to attend Islamic classes, even as children. In addition to these, we had a special teacher come to our home to teach us the Qur'an and the Arabic language. I completed reading the entire Qur'an and memorized a large part of it by the age of thirteen. I carried out all my religious duties faithfully and was even filled with joy in doing so. My father diligently taught me how to pray. Every time I mispronounced a word in the recitation of the Qur'an, my dad corrected me. Every time I performed the prayers, he was by my side, guiding me. My dad taught me that "Islam is not only your faith, but also your lifestyle, your family. Islam is our way of life. Islam is our relationships. Our belief in Allah and His Prophet should not just be in our hearts; it must pervade all aspects of our lives—our family, our standard of living, all relationships, our passions, and everything that we do."

Sitting in that park, lonely and reflecting on my life, I was trying to calm my tumultuous mind by calling on the *Asma-ul-husna*—the ninety-nine beautiful names of Allah. The word Islam is derived from the Arabic word for peace (*salaam*), and as I called on the name of Allah, I searched for peace that now eluded me. I continually recited *surah* after *surah* (chapters in the Qur'an) and many *duas* (prayers) that I had learned. Yet the turmoil inside was unceasing.

My thoughts turned to my school life. I have cherished memories of my school life, even up to today. My father wanted me to obtain a good education, better than all my relatives. He always desired the best for me and, therefore, enrolled me in a very good school run by Anglo-Indians where English was the medium of instruction. Speaking English was considered very prestigious; because of former British rule, English became one of the official languages of India. I cherished the school activities. There were debates, skits, extemporaneous speeches, charade competitions, literary skill contests, and much more, in addition to the standard curriculum. Above all, I had many friends, whom I think of often.

In this school, I had many opportunities to hear about Jesus. During the Christmas season, the school hosted people from all over the country, who performed many skits, songs, and mimes, primarily about the birth of Jesus into this world. Sometimes visitors shared stories of the great men of God from the Bible and, in the end, gave away free Gideon New Testaments. At home, I tried reading it once but did not understand because it was in old, formal English. When my father saw me reading it, he grabbed it from me and threw it in a box, which he put, along with old and useless things, in the loft of our house. Afterward, he cautioned me often regarding Christianity and its followers, saying, "Never trust the Christians. They are all liars. They have twisted the message about Jesus. Jesus was not God; he was just a man of God, a prophet whom Allah favored. Therefore, you watch out for people who tell you that He is God. Beware of such blasphemy." He frequently supported his stance with the following verse from the Qur'an:

> *There is among them a section who distort the Book with their tongues; (as they read) so that you would think it is a part of the Book, but it is no part of the Book; and they say, 'That is from Allah,' but it is not from Allah: it is they who tell a lie against Allah and (well) they know it!*—Surat al Imran (3):78

One day, he called me to his side and asked, "When you pass from one grade to another, do you read the books of the lower grades?"

I said, "No, I don't need them."

He said, "Precisely. Just as you don't need books of the second or third grade when you come to your tenth grade, so also you don't need the previous revelations given to other prophets before Muhammad because they are outdated and have been superseded by the Qur'an, which is the final revelation from Allah."

My ambition in life was to become a doctor and treat people who were helpless, sick, and needy. I tried my best to study well, and I was only a few months away from entering a medical college to fulfill my dream. Now this great turmoil in our family was threatening my life's ambition, and there was no way this problem could be solved. As I sat in the park, I looked back at where it all started.

My father was from southern India, and my mother was from the western part of India. Their families met, I should say, through divine providence. My dad was about thirty-five years old and my mom only seventeen when their families arranged their marriage. It was a common practice in our religion to marry a bride of a much younger age. Our family was small and tightly knit. We were well-to-do and had all we wanted. We owned a house with a beautiful garden surrounding it. My father provided well for our family; however, he was a short-tempered man. There were occasional fights between my father and mother. I had gotten used to it. My father believed that beating was the best way to right the wrongs in children and wives. Over the previous few years, this had escalated, and my father was becoming increasingly short-tempered. One night the situation got out of hand, and my father beat my mother until she started bleeding. The next day our relatives came to our home and tried to counsel my parents. Nevertheless, the incidents increased. I could not understand what was wrong between them.

What had driven me to the park this evening was another incident between my father and mother. The verbal deluge turned into a fistfight, and my father began beating my mother. While this was going on, I entered the house from school and saw the whole scene. In the heat of the moment, with my mother reeling in pain and my raging father preparing to punch her, I intervened and tried to hold him back. His anger turned toward me, and he started beating me.

After tempers subsided, my father announced that he was going to divorce my mother and send his children away with her because they were disrespectful and disobedient. When I heard those words, my whole world came crashing down. The thought of having to live in poverty, of not being able to complete my education and fulfill my life's ambition, was just too much. After a few hours, I quietly left home, determined never to return or at least never to return alive. Rather than waiting to see how wretched life would become as a result of the events that had just taken place, I decided to end this misery by ending my life.

"Into His Marvelous Light"

1 Peter 2:9

Still seated in that park, I gazed at my watch. It was well past 10:00 p.m. The more I thought of the separation of my parents, the more I was fed up with life. I just could not go on with all the turmoil raging around me. I started thinking of different ways to commit suicide. I wanted it to be easy. I wanted to be at peace, at least in my death. Therefore, I contemplated which way I was going to bring an end to my miserable life.

As my mind was preoccupied with thoughts of suicide, I heard a voice—not one inside my head but an audible voice, strong and powerful yet serene and gentle. The voice called me by name and said, "Try Me. I am Jesus."

As I heard this voice, a sense of calm spread over me. The suicidal feeling instantly vanished. I had never felt so filled with peace.

Almost immediately, my mind filled with questions. I was sure what I had heard was not my imagination, because the peace I felt was real. Nevertheless, my mind was questioning, "Why am I hearing this voice?" "Whose voice is this?" "Why is this voice speaking to me, and how does this voice speak my name?" "How can I follow Jesus, since I am a Muslim and he is only a prophet?" Question after question bombarded my mind. As my head throbbed with all those queries, a memory from two years earlier surfaced like a faint light from the darkness.

Because of my ambition to become a doctor, biology had been my favorite subject. My tenth-grade biology teacher was good, and I admired her for her intellect. She was also a deeply religious Hindu. She kept all the duties of her religion. She always wore a red dot on her forehead, a bit bigger than others', which I thought was an attempt to show off the depth of her Hindu religious beliefs. One day she came to school without the red dot on her forehead. In Hindu society, the only woman who does not wear a red dot is a widow. As she entered the school compound, I noticed this and ran to her, wanting to express my heartfelt condolences.

As I expressed my regrets at her loss, she stopped me in midsentence, saying her husband was well. I asked her why she was not wearing the red dot. She replied, "Because I am not a Hindu anymore. I am a child of Jesus. One night I saw a vision of Jesus. I saw Him clearly, and He lifted me out of the miry clay, washed me, and made me whole, cleansing me from all my infirmities and sins. I realized that Jesus came into this world to die for my sins and that I need not be ashamed anymore; I have assurance of being with Jesus when this life is over." She spoke of Jesus as if He was there with her, walking with her, talking with her, and taking care of her in the most personal way that I had ever seen. I was totally dumbstruck.

For me this was blasphemy to the core. I was furious. I said, "You cannot be worshipping Jesus, who is just a man. He was a prophet. How can you call him God? This is blasphemy!" The color drained from my face, and a multitude of feelings overcame me. I liked this teacher very much, and seeing her following something that I thought was not right made my heart sink. I distinctly remember trying to reason with her, arguing that according to the Qur'an, Jesus was not God but just a man whom God had favored. I told her that she was making a big mistake and would soon regret the disgrace and shame that she was bringing upon herself.

After many long moments of discussion, she finally said (and the words still ring fresh in my ears), "Syed, you may not understand what I am going through right now, yet a day will come when you will comprehend this mystery. I will be praying for you until such a day that God will reveal himself to you."

As this two-year-old memory flooded my mind, I heard the same voice again, saying, "Try Me. I am Jesus." I had goose bumps all over my body. I sensed a powerful presence entirely engulf my being. The voice called me again by name and said, "Try Me. I am Jesus." Three times I heard this voice.

Though my heart and mind filled with peace, the questions in my mind about this Jesus continued. The first and foremost was, "Who is this Jesus, and why should I follow Him?" I was at a loss for answers, and I was feeling very impatient. Suddenly, I realized that my former biology teacher was the one that I needed to contact to answer all my questions. I did not delay a bit. I knew where she lived, since I had once helped carry schoolbooks to her house.

Voices conflicted in my head. One voice told me that it was a very bad idea. Another said that I should not be too concerned, that it was not very important, and that it was probably just my tired mind playing games. Still another voice said I should wait until the morning and not immediately pursue it. However, an overwhelming sense of urgency pushed me forward to meet with her right then.

I glanced at my watch. It was past 10:30 p.m., and I remembered that the next day was Christmas. I was sure her family would be busy, but I could not shake the overwhelming urgency to visit immediately. I rushed to her house.

The house was serene and quiet. As I stood outside the door for a few minutes, eerie voices in my head debated and tried to convince me that this was a foolish idea, that maybe they did not live there anymore, or that maybe they were all asleep. Still other voices said my teacher might not welcome me inside or might not be of any help. These voices grew unbearably loud, but then a sudden sense of purpose filled my mind, and I rang the doorbell. I felt like a complete fool ringing someone's doorbell at nearly midnight.

My teacher opened the door and was surprised to see me standing there. "Oh, Syed, what a pleasant surprise! Come in; come in." I went in timidly, and we exchanged traditional greetings. It was Christmas Eve, so they were preparing for the next day. Even so, she and her family welcomed me warmly into their home. I was embarrassed to start the conversation for which I had come, so I nervously chattered about other things.

Sensing in her spirit that I was there for some important reason, my teacher said, "Okay, Syed, stop all this beating around the bush, and tell me why you have come here today. What happened?" I was surprised by the fact that she felt there was something I wanted to share. I told her everything that had happened from earlier that evening up until the present. She listened to it all intently and then said, "Since you heard the voice of Jesus, which is clear from the detailed account that you gave, I want to tell you that Jesus has placed an invitation before you to follow Him. It is your choice whether you accept it or reject it. As for the other voices in your head, well, they are evil forces trying to stop you from understanding the truth."

She explained the good news of Jesus Christ to me once again, as she had two years previously. She said that when the first man, Adam, disobeyed God, not only did he become separated from God due to his sin but guilt, shame, and fear entered his life as well. God does not look on sin or tolerate sin. At the same time, He does not want humans to be ashamed in front of Him nor live in fear. God desired to restore humans to the same unbroken relationship that Adam and Eve had with Him in the Garden of Eden. However, He is just; therefore, sin must be punished.

My teacher explained that the Bible says,

> *The wages of sin is death, but the gift of God is eternal life in Christ Jesus our Lord.* —Romans 6:23

> *But God demonstrates His own love for us in this: While we were still sinners, Christ died for us.* —Romans 5:8

God sent Jesus Christ, His Son, to this earth to receive the judgment due to man. Jesus lived on earth for thirty-three years; bore the punishment for our sins, our shamefulness, and our fears; and died on the cross because of the great love He has for us. However, demonstrating His victory over sin, Satan, and death, He rose again on the third day, and He is at the right hand of God interceding for us. Whoever believes in Him will have eternal life (see John 3:16). Jesus takes from us not only our sin, but also the shame, guilt, and fear of eternal separation from God. Now we can have the assurance that we will be with Jesus forever, when our earthly life is over. With many other verses from the Bible, she shared the incredibly good news of Jesus, and she patiently answered my questions.

It was as if my eyes suddenly opened to the truth previously hidden from me, truth I had been unable to comprehend. She invited me to come to the church the next day, since it was Christmas. I agreed to be there on time, and I left. On the way back home, I was contemplating the truth I had heard from her about Jesus, His love, His sacrifice on the cross, and His resurrection. Tears flowed like a flood down my cheeks. I wondered why I did not comprehend when she told me these things two years ago, and I was very upset at my Islamic scholars and teachers for not telling me the truth. I felt as if all I knew about my religion was shaken to the core—my beliefs, my faith, and even my zeal for Islam and Allah were suddenly, utterly meaningless. I was ashamed of myself for being a sinner and living a life of shame.

Born to Die

The next day, I left my house without telling anyone where I was going. The church was not difficult to find, since it was the biggest building in that area. A mixture of feelings welled up inside me as I entered. Fear was the primary one. I did not want anyone who knew me to see me entering a church. Next came doubt about whether what I was doing was right or if it would result in dishonor and shame. But, I also felt excitement to see and know more of the truth for myself.

Upon entering the church, I was surprised to see everyone standing and singing praises to God—and with much joy. My religious leaders had always taught me that Christians displayed pictures or idols in their churches and were worshippers of Mary, the mother of Jesus, and other human beings who were called saints. But to my surprise, I looked around and saw no images, idols, or pictures of Jesus. My teacher approached me as I was standing in a corner near the entrance. She led me by my hand to the front of the church. It was a surreal experience for me. I had never been in a place of worship with so much noise. In the mosques, generally, there was "pin-drop silence." This was a religious cultural shock to me. Yet the joy and peace on the faces of the people were almost tangible and contagious. I felt a strange feeling of peace pervade my whole being. The voice that had spoken to me the night before was still ringing in my ears. A sense of assurance swept over me, calming my fear, nervousness, and doubt. I had never felt that kind of peace in all my life. I had been taught that Islam is the religion of peace. Every time we greeted each other, we would say, *salaam-u-aleikkum* (peace be upon you). But this peace I was experiencing in church was not of words, not outward calm or silence but inward peace, which no human words could properly express. And in that instant, I knew I had to follow the way of Jesus.

The pastor's Christmas message shocked me. I expected him to tell of the birth of Jesus. Instead, he spoke about the death of Jesus. He said, "The birth of Jesus cannot be isolated from His death on the cross. Jesus was born to die—to die for you and for me. He shed His blood and died in order to deliver us from sin, suffering, shame, and eternity in hell. He rose from the grave on the third day to show us that He won the victory over death and Satan, and anyone who believes in Him will have everlasting life."

I made my decision, right there and then, to commit the rest of my life to Jesus and follow Him. I asked Jesus to forgive all my sins, deliver me from shame, and accept me as His child. Peace that surpasses all understanding filled me inside and out. Unspeakable joy pervaded my soul. I felt the loving presence of the Lord Jesus with me, and I knew that all my sins were forgiven, that I need not be ashamed of entering His presence, and that I now had a place reserved for me in heaven.

"Life in Christ Jesus"

II Timothy 3:12

I went home that day a changed and transformed person. It was clear to me that if my parents and my friends came to know about this, they would not be pleased. According to Islam, I had done a most shameful thing and had committed an unforgivable sin—I had forsaken Islam and become an infidel.

> *O prophet! Strive hard against the unbelievers and the hypocrites, and be firm against them.*—Surat at Tauba (9):73

> *And if any of you turn back from their faith and die in unbelief, their works will bear no*

fruit in this life and in the Hereafter: they will be companions of the Fire and will abide therein.—Surat al Baqaraa (2):217

I knew that neither my parents nor my relatives nor the leaders of the mosque would approve of my actions. If they came to know, I was sure it would be a lonely, tough, and troubled road ahead. Therefore, I decided to keep my newfound faith a secret. Each week, on the day of worship, I left my home on the pretext of visiting my friends and instead went to the church. The Lord was with me during that time, and He spoke to me continually. When the Lord spoke to me that I should be baptized, I approached my pastor and shared my desire. About a month after I first came to Jesus, I was baptized in the church.

I read in the Bible that the Holy Spirit led Jesus into the wilderness to fast and pray for forty days. Challenged by this, I decided to spend time in fasting and prayer. In the next forty days, I completed reading the whole Bible, relishing every single word. It enriched my soul. The Lord began speaking to me about the various aspects of my life that needed transformation. I took great pleasure in spending time in prayer and reading His Word.

By that time, my father's ongoing anger had caused him to throw my mother, my sister, and me out of the house.

We were reduced to poverty and were living in a small hut with only one room for all of us. I thought that having lived in luxury, this life of poverty would be a misery. But to my amazement, the joy of Christ in my heart never diminished, and I found myself relishing every moment that I spent with Jesus.

"Persecuted"

II Timothy 3:12

After my baptism, I received a certificate of baptism with my name written on it in bold letters. I did not want it and did not know what to do with it. So I just folded it and left it amid my schoolbooks. I now realize that it is a very bad idea to give a certificate of baptism to a Muslim who has recently come to Jesus, and it is even worse if that Muslim-background believer is living in a Muslim neighborhood.

One day while my mother was cleaning the house, she happened to come across that certificate of baptism. I had many certificates that I had won through many competitions, and she thought that it was something important. She did not know much English, but she knew enough to read and understand. As she read it, she was horrified.

Returning home that evening, I saw a large number of shoes outside my house. I instantly knew that something had happened and that I was in trouble. I quickly uttered a prayer for protection and wisdom from the Lord. I felt the presence of Jesus close by my side. When I entered the single room of the house, there was a big crowd. It was comprised of my uncles, aunts, near and far relatives, friends, and the elders from the mosque I had frequented just a few months prior.

I knew immediately that my "secret life with Jesus" was now public. Utter chaos ruled as I entered the room. Some of my relatives were shouting at me, some started beating me with their fists, and others called me an infidel who had committed shameful acts. The older women were sitting in a corner, wailing loudly and mourning for the acts that I had committed, yet a few other aunts of mine tried to protect me from the barrage of blows and spoke to me lovingly. The elders of the mosque sat in one corner quietly taking in all that was happening in front of their eyes.

After the initial fury had subsided, I was forced to sit in their midst. My relatives started asking me many questions. "Why did you do such a shameful thing?" one of my uncles asked.

My cousins said, "You have disgraced not only yourself but also all of us. No one in our world has ever heard of such a thing that you have done."

My aunt tried to coerce a reply out of me and asked, "Did the Christians promise you much wealth, did they promise you a prosperous future in some western country, or have you just gone mad to forsake Islam and follow an inferior path?"

There was again a barrage of physical blows from someone, and one relative pulled the assailant back from me. The elders of the mosque began talking. One said that by forsaking Islam, which is "the straight path," I had brought down a curse not only upon myself but also upon my family. Another said that when someone forsakes Islam, the Hadith commands us to kill that person.

> *For the prophet said, "if somebody (a Muslim) discards his religion, kill him"* — Sahih Bukhari, Vol. 4, Book 52, #260

Some of my uncles started threatening me by saying that I might end up being killed if I continued down the same path. The elders insisted that the Christians are deceitful people who are themselves deceived by lies. They declared again from the Qur'an that God is one and cannot have a son. I had been taught this hundreds of times before.

> *Say: He is Allah, the One; Allah, the Eternal, Absolute; He begetteth not, nor is He begotten; And there is none like unto Him.* —Surat al Ikhlaas (112):1–4

They asserted that the Bible, which the Christians believe in, is corrupted to the core and does not contain an ounce of truth. They also said that the Christians worship not one but three gods, which is considered *shirk*, an unforgivable sin of associating partners with Allah. They said many other such things, trying to dissuade me from following Jesus and force me back to Islam. They also gave me many books written by Ahmed Deedat and other local Muslim authors from our country, which proclaimed similar things about the Christian faith. I read them all in the days that followed.

This "interrogation" lasted for nearly six hours. Since it was close to midnight, many of them left, only because they were tired. I knew this would continue. As I read through all the books, the Lord Jesus guarded my heart and helped me stand firm in Him. While reading all the objections of Ahmed Deedat, who totally degraded the Christian faith, I felt confused at times and sometimes doubtful as to whether I had made the right decision. Whenever the doubts came, the voice that I had heard in the park resounded in my ears, "Try Me. I am Jesus," and an assurance settled over my confused heart that I was, indeed, walking on the right path.

These meetings in our house continued for the next three years. Initially every day, at least one of my relatives and the elders of the mosque were present. Eventually, there were weekly meetings. Then they occurred once every few weeks. Every meeting was typical of the first one, characterized by physical beatings, calling down curses, threats, advice, and the like. I became used to these things.

On one particular occasion, one of my cousins sprang to his feet, placed a knife at my throat, and threatened to slash it if I did not return to Islam right then. But one of my uncles pulled him off me and sent him away. The Lord protected my life through all of this persecution, which He had somehow considered me worthy to endure. Not only that, He also strengthened my spirit every single day. I always felt His loving presence so close to me; His marvelous grace sustaining me; His powerful Word encouraging me; and His Holy Spirit guiding my every step, giving me words of wisdom to speak at appropriate moments. I felt His mighty strength coursing through me in my weakness. His victory was mine in temptations. I experienced His miraculous protection in persecution, His divine providence meeting my needs, and His never-failing love and care holding me in His sweet embrace.

As I read the books, which were intended to bring me back to Islam, the Lord was teaching me many things that would be useful in the future for reaching out to Muslims with the truth of the gospel and the love of Jesus. I read and researched in order to answer the objections and queries raised by Muslims.

Persecution at Home

As the persecution from my relatives continued, the situation at home deteriorated. My mother and sister were angry at the prospect of me, an infidel, staying under the same roof with them. As I mentioned earlier, we were living in a house that was only a single room, so I did not make my prayer life public. I always prayed in the middle of the night. I did this so as not to aggravate the anger of my mother and my sister. I made sure they were sleeping soundly and then knelt on my sleeping mat and prayed silently. One night, as I was praying, my sister got up and switched on the lights. Apparently, they had been observing me. When they saw what I was doing, both my mother and my sister got very angry and beat me severely. My sister kicked me, and they stripped off my clothes and threw me out of the house in just my undergarments. It was almost 1:00 a.m., and I was standing outside the house. As an eighteen-year-old teenage boy, I was embarrassed and ashamed. My body shivered but not from cold. On the contrary, it was warm and humid. The shivering was due to my shame at being nearly naked. I said a prayer to the Lord to help me and give me the strength that I needed to go through this situation victoriously.

I knocked and called to them repeatedly to open the door and have mercy on me. But they were adamant in their decision and said, "We will open the door only if you promise not to worship this Jesus." However, this was the one demand with which I could not comply. How could I, after knowing the truth, refrain from walking in it and deny it? I stood there for more than an hour, knocking intermittently. Yet, there was no response from inside the house. The lights were eventually switched off, and I assumed that they had gone to sleep with no intention of opening the door.

I then decided to walk to the church. India is always lively, and people are on the streets during all hours of the night. I am sure the people who saw me in my undergarments thought I was an insane man needing help. Many averted their gaze from me. I prayed to the Lord to help me and immediately felt a strength surge through my body. I felt the comforting presence of the Lord engulf me, and I was no longer ashamed of my nakedness. I walked the four-kilometer stretch to the church and slept in the hall. I lived there for a couple of months. The pastor did not mind my staying there. It was refreshing to be in the church. During that time, the Lord strengthened me. My family members searched for me and finally discovered that I had gone to the church. Some of my uncles and aunts visited me when I was in the church and compelled me to return home. They shamed me by saying that I had left two helpless women alone at home with no one to care for or support them. They said I was a coward to leave all my family responsibilities and run away from them. They repeatedly insisted that I return home and take care of my mom and younger sister. I had no choice and was pressured to return home.

Nonetheless, upon my return, their angry attitude and beatings continued.

One or more members of my family or the elders from the mosque persistently visited me. They adopted many ways of persuasion—counseling, advising, beating, threatening, and trying to lure me back to Islam through marriage to one of their daughters. They even attributed my family's problems to Allah cursing them because of my actions.

Persecution in College

By this time I had finished my school studies and wanted to attend college but was unable to because of my financial situation. Since my father had abandoned us, it was difficult to make both ends meet. Though I was not able to pursue my dream of becoming a doctor, I still was very happy in Jesus. I applied for a bachelor's program at several Christian colleges in my city but all refused admission to me because I did not have enough money to pay. Then one of my uncles helped me apply to a college that was run by an Islamic administration. The principal of the college reviewed my application and immediately granted me admission to the bachelor of zoology program, even though I did not have the necessary funds to pay and classes had already begun a month earlier. My uncle took this opportunity to explain to me that it was the Muslims who cared for my welfare, and he asked me to return to Islam. On one hand, I was happy to be able to pursue this bachelor's degree, but on the other hand, I was sad that I had to study in a college run by a Muslim administration. I had thought that gaining admission to a college run by a Christian administration would mean I could be in fellowship with godly people and could grow in the Lord. But I realized later that the Lord does everything with a purpose and leads His children in accordance with His will. Many a time, we do not understand His higher purposes, yet He never stops fulfilling His will in the lives of His children. Jesus wanted me to be a witness for Him in the college where I was studying. In my class of fifty students, forty-five were Muslims and only one was a follower of Jesus—me! It was a wonderful opportunity to show the love of Jesus to my friends. Nevertheless, the task was not at all easy. On the contrary, it was dangerous, as I was soon to discover.

Word spread about me to all the Muslims in the area and eventually reached the college where I was studying. At this time, I was working part-time in a mobile restaurant to pay for my studies and to take care of my mother and my sister. I used to invite my classmates to this mobile restaurant. It was a demanding job and I hardly had time left for my studies, but Jesus gave me the strength I needed to continue. That November, we had our first semester exams. The Lord in His absolute mercy helped me to achieve top grades in all my subjects. All my friends and classmates were surprised by this and asked how I was able to do so well while working so many hours. We sat down in the college canteen, about ten of us, and I told them that it was possible only because of the sheer grace of God. I also shared about Jesus, His great love and sacrifice for us on the cross, as well as my encounter with Him in the park the previous year. I told them that I was a follower of Jesus and extended an invitation to all of them to follow Jesus.

Many of my friends had already heard that I was now a follower of Jesus but were waiting for an opportunity to hear it from my own mouth. As I was sharing with them, I saw a change come over their countenances. They were becoming extremely agitated and angry. They were so furious that some of them left without saying a word, while a few others started shouting obscene words at me for forsaking Islam and becoming a *kafir*, a pagan. From that day on, I had a lot of trouble from my classmates. They would simply beat me up for no reason or steal my books. I had expected persecution, but what I endured was far worse. In the midst of all this, the Lord was with me and gave me the strength I needed.

It did not stop there. Most of my professors were Muslims, and they had heard from the mosque that I used to attend that I was now following Jesus instead of Islam. The professors who had held me in high regard because I was at the top of my class now wanted to put me down. Some of them called me to their offices and counseled me, saying that I was going down a wrong path. The principal of the college warned me that if I did not correct my path, they would dismiss me from the college. My friends ignored me and continued to ridicule and beat me on occasion. My professors were trying their best to fail me in internal evaluations so that I would not complete the course. Yet the Lord was good and sustained me through all these struggles.

One day, a group of my classmates joined together and dragged me by my leg to the mosque inside the college campus. They mocked me, beat me, and pushed me inside to perform the Friday prayers. In all of this, Jesus gave me the grace and strength to stand up to them firmly. I told them resolutely that I would not perform the ceremonial ablution, or *wudu*, which is required to enter the mosque. My friends then kicked me in the gut and left me there while they performed their prayers. The Lord delivered me that day from their hands.

My uncles appointed a person to follow me and report all that I did. Even though I was going through all this, I felt the personal presence of the Lord Jesus Christ with me all the time. His strength and grace coursed through my veins, and I felt His protection around me. It was, indeed, a joy to carry the cross of Christ. The Lord never allowed any real harm to come to me.

"But We Trust in the Lord"

Psalm 20:7

As the persecution continued for the next three years, it became difficult for me to continue my studies. My college mates were becoming increasingly hostile, to the point that I had to discontinue my college studies in my final year. However, I was not saddened by it. On the contrary, an unspeakable joy filled me. Many of my friends and family members said I was a fool to ruin my life by following this Jesus. But for me, my Lord Jesus was everything. I would give up anything for His sake.

Amid all this, as I spent time with the Lord, I clearly sensed His call upon my life to serve Him by taking the message of Jesus to the people who have not heard about Him. I committed my life to serve Him. Jesus took away my sin and shame, and now I could approach the presence of God boldly. I felt that all the peoples of this earth should have an opportunity to hear the message of the cross. Therefore, I grabbed every chance to go out and share the good news. Every weekend I went out with teams to share about Jesus to many people. Along with three of my friends, I went to the beach both in the morning and evening to distribute printed material about Jesus and explain the good news of Jesus to all those who asked of us. The thought that my people, the Muslims, would spend eternity away from the presence of God added an increased fervency to my efforts. Being filled with a deep love and burden for my people, I traveled to various places, sharing the message of the love of Jesus with many. As my pastor realized the call upon my life, he suggested I go to a Bible college to study and prepare myself for the work of the Lord.

At his suggestion, I applied to a Bible college in another city and, by the grace of God, gained admission there for the bachelor of theology program. But I was astounded when I looked at the tuition fees—they were enormous. With the boarding, lodging, and other expenses, it would be a mammoth amount for me. I did not have the resources to pay such fees, and I could not imagine that my family members would even think of supporting me in this venture. I approached the pastor for his help. I asked if he could help me pay my fees for the next three years. The pastor replied with a question, "Syed, why are you going to the Bible college?"

I replied, "To prepare myself for the work of the Lord, to learn more about the Bible, and to learn to share the good news effectively."

Then my pastor asked, "Who called you for this work?"

I said without an inkling of doubt, "The Lord Jesus called me."

Then he said, "You know, if Jesus has called you for His work, then probably you should ask Him to take care of your needs rather than approaching me."

Initially, I was very saddened by what he said. The pastor knew I had no resources whatsoever, and I was shattered when he said he would not support me. Nevertheless, he did it with all good intentions. As I came to know later, he wanted me to learn the very important lesson of trusting in God rather than men. I thought of asking help from a few church believers whom I knew to be very compassionate. Coming down the stairs of the church, I encountered a brother who said, "Syed, I heard that you are off to a Bible college to prepare for ministry. I want to help you. I will send a small amount every month to take care of your personal needs." I was excited and thanked him for his generosity.

Later on, a sister from our home Bible-study group came to me and said, "Brother Syed, we want to help you in your studies, so we are planning to collect a monthly offering in our group to send to you each month. It should be enough to pay your fees." I was thrilled to hear this, thrilled that even though the pastor did not want to support me, the church believers were more than willing. So I thanked the brother and the sister for their help and gave them the address of the Bible college that I was going to so that they could send the necessary funds at the right time.

Eager to study the Word of God, I went to the Bible college with a resolve to apply myself to my studies and do my best. In addition to my studies, I had many opportunities to join with others in seeking out Muslims in order to share with them how Jesus had changed our lives.

However, the Lord was teaching me something. A month after I came to the Bible college, I was expecting to receive some financial help from the brother and sister who had made a promise to me. I waited and waited. A month went by and then two. I received neither funds from them nor any information. I was becoming concerned. I thought they might have forgotten, so I wrote a letter to each of them. (Emails and cell phones were not common at that time in our location.) I received no response. Month after month passed, and day after day I awaited the arrival of the postman to bring me news, but nothing happened. My first semester was drawing to a close, and I was troubled. Only after clearing all the outstanding fees would I be allowed to write the exams at the end of the semester. I began to question the Lord as to why this was happening. How can people forget the promise they made? A feeling of desperation came over me.

Monday was my exam, and it was already Friday. The postman came and went for the day. I did not know what to do. As I was fretting over the situation, the voice of my pastor rang in my ears. "You know, if Jesus has called you for His work, then probably you should ask Him to take care of your needs rather than approaching me." I realized that although in the past few months I had been praying to the Lord, never once did I pray to Him for any of my needs, including my fees. I was so caught up in the promises of men that I had neglected to look to the Lord for that particular need.

I decided to fast and pray the next day and commit myself once again to the Lord. I excused myself from the weekend ministry and headed out to the woods opposite our Bible college. There was a tree under which I used to spend many hours praying to the Lord. Early that Saturday morning, I headed out to that place, cried out to the Lord, and asked for His forgiveness for not trusting in Him. I confessed my lack of faith in Him and surrendered my life to Him once again. I told Jesus that I did not have anyone to count on except Him.

By two o'clock in the afternoon, the Lord spoke. The same voice that spoke to me in the park now spoke powerfully to me again, saying, "My son, go in peace. Since you renewed your trust in Me, I will do mighty works in your life." I knew at once that the Lord was in control, and I chided myself for the folly of trusting in man. I finished my prayer with thanks and went back to the campus. As I arrived, one of my professors called me and asked me to meet him in his office. I usually ran some errands for the professors, so I thought that he had some work for me. As I entered his office, he handed over an envelope and said, "Syed, the Lord spoke to me this morning to give you an offering. So here it is." I was astonished. I was praying to Jesus in the morning, and He had already started working even as I was praying. I prayed a blessing over my professor and went to my room to open the envelope. I saw that it contained a check for half the amount of my fees. I was thrilled and went straight to the bursar's office to pay the fees. I realized, that day, how true the Word of God is:

> *Those who look to Him are radiant; their faces are never covered with shame.—*
> Psalm 34:5

As the bursar took my fees, he asked when I would pay the rest of it. Faith welled up inside of me and I told him, "Sir, just as the Lord sent ravens to feed Elijah in the desert, so also the Lord has sent a raven to meet my needs. Those who trust in the Lord will never be ashamed, and He will send another raven this way, very soon." A few minutes after I spoke, another professor walked into the office, presented another check for the remaining amount, and paid my fees. It all happened so quickly, that I stood there dumbstruck. The Lord truly takes care of us when we put our trust in Him.

> *Some trust in chariots and some in horses, but we trust in the name of the Lord our God.—*Psalm 20:7

From that day on, the Lord never put me to shame. Many a time I did not even know who had paid my fees. The Lord took care of every need. When I went to the Lord with my need, He always performed a miracle, speaking to His servants to help me. With all my financial woes taken care of, I was able to fully devote myself to study. The Lord helped me excel in my studies and be first in my class.

"Who Shall Separate Us from the Love of Christ"

Romans 8:35

It was the end of the first year of studies in the Bible college, and I was supposed to go back to my hometown for summer ministry. As I prepared to leave, I got the information that my father, who had left us many years earlier, was searching for me. I decided to go meet him. I felt a great burden for him in my heart and wanted to share the truth with him. I got his new address from one of our relatives and set out.

When I located the address, I found that it was a big mansion he had newly built. As I entered, I saw a nameplate engraved on the front of the house. It had my name on it, the name by which my father called me. I was thrilled to see that he had named the house after me. I went inside, and he welcomed me very warmly, embraced me, and shed many a tear, saying it had been very unwise of him to leave us all. He said that he longed to be with his family once again. I was very happy at this turn of events. He invited our relatives and his friends and arranged a big feast. It was a joyful reunion. I recognized that God had worked a miracle, and I praised Him for it.

At the end of the feast, when all our guests had left, my father sat down with me and inquired of my state of affairs, about what I was doing and where I had been while he had not been able to locate me. I saw this as an opportunity to share about Jesus. I told him of how I met the Lord and that I was presently involved in preparation for His work. He was visibly shocked and agitated at this. He said, "All these untoward incidences have occurred just because I have neglected my responsibilities as a father. It is because of my failure that you have strayed away from Islam." He then asked for my forgiveness and said that he would like to make amends. He said that he wanted now to reunite with the family and that we could all live together in the new mansion. I was delighted at the thought of being together again.

He then offered, "Syed, I have built this mansion for you. It bears your name right in the front. I hope that you have already seen it. I want you to be happy and content all of your life. I have so much wealth that there will be no need for you to ever work. Even your grandchildren will have enough to live on with what I have. I am planning to give all of my inheritance to you. I will transfer everything that I have to you. I want you to live happily without any struggle in your life. I just want you to do one thing. Will you do it for me?"

He said this in a most solemn tone and in a very loving manner, yet as he said it, there came a feeling of uneasiness inside me. I knew what he was intending. I said, "Tell me, father."

He continued, "I just want you to leave that Bible college, come back to Islam, and stay with me. I want to spend the rest of my life with you by my side. I know that what I am asking is not much when compared to all that I will do for you. But will you do it?" My heart sank inside me, and I felt all my strength draining from me. I knew that my father loved me a great deal, and I also knew that this was a very good offer. If I did accept it, I would have no worries or cares and would live luxuriously for the rest of my life. On the other hand, how could I forsake my relationship with Jesus, who had demonstrated His love for me by dying on the cross? I was at a loss for words. I was being torn between the love of my earthly father and the love of my heavenly Father.

Then my father said, "There is no need for you to answer me now. Think about it. Analyze all the implications of your decision wisely, and answer me in the morning. But I expect a favorable answer from you. You know that I care for you and do not want you to suffer any more in life. I just want the best for you. So think and decide." He left me to ponder the matter. I started praying to Jesus to help me in this situation. I did not want to offend my father, yet I did not want to turn my back on Jesus.

I telephoned one of the Christian brothers I knew and told him about what my father had proposed, asking him for suggestions. He said, "Syed, as I see it, this is a very good opportunity for you. You do not want to lose your father's love or this offer that has been placed before you. If you lose your father's trust now, you will never be able to regain it and will never be able to share the love of Jesus with him. Therefore, take what your dad has to offer. Leave the Bible college; you can continue your studies at a later time. Tell your father that you will stay with him, and if possible, come to the church once in a while when your father does not know. You do not need to tell anyone what happened inside your house. After your father transfers all his inheritance to you, and after his life on earth is over, then you can continue doing the Lord's work and can be a blessing to many people with the wealth that you have. You see, God's word says that you have to be innocent as doves but also wise as serpents. So, be wise and make the best use of the wonderful opportunity that God has placed before you."

When I heard those words, a strange voice inside of me said that it was a very wise suggestion this brother had given. It would not offend my father. I would still be able to work, sharing about Jesus secretly until my father passed away, and then I would be able to be a blessing to many. Though my mind repeatedly told me this was the best course of action to take, I was greatly troubled in my spirit. The peace of the Lord, which had engulfed me, seemed far off now. I was in a dilemma as to whether to please my earthly father or to please my Father in heaven. I decided to go to the Lord for His ever-present help and beseech Him for His guidance.

I went to the rooftop of that mansion and prayed to the Lord to help me in this situation. After I prayed for a while, the Lord spoke. He reminded me of a verse in the New Testament.

> *But whatever was to my profit I now consider loss for the sake of Christ.*— Philippians 3:7

The Lord said, "This enormous wealth might indeed profit you, but will you be able to consider it loss for my sake? Just remember that I gave up my heavenly abode for you and came down to redeem you. Will you be able to do the same? The choice is ultimately yours."

As the Word of the Lord hit me, I was instantly reminded of other passages in the Bible. In Matthew, Satan tempted Jesus, saying,

> *"All this I will give you," he said, "if you will bow down and worship me." Jesus said to him, "Away from me, Satan! For it is written: 'Worship the Lord your God and serve him only.'"*—Matthew 4:9–10

The Lord also reminded me that Satan used Bible verses to tempt Jesus; likewise, the Christian brother had used Bible verses to appear as if he were giving godly advice. Furthermore, the Spirit of the Lord brought to mind these verses from the Bible:

> *Who shall separate us from the love of Christ? Shall trouble or hardship or persecution or famine or nakedness or danger or sword? As it is written: 'For your sake we face death all day long; we are considered as sheep to be slaughtered.'*

No, in all these things we are more than conquerors through him who loved us. For I am convinced that neither death nor life, neither angels nor demons, neither the present nor the future, nor any powers, neither height nor depth, nor anything else in all creation, will be able to separate us from the love of God that is in Christ Jesus our Lord.—Romans 8:35–39

I broke down immediately. I knew that I should have made the decision to follow Jesus as soon as my father made his offer. In a moment of temptation and weakness, had the Lord not helped me, I probably would have a made a wrong decision. I asked the Lord to forgive my weakness. I had been on the verge of turning my back on the one who had loved me with eternal love. I would have started living a hypocritical life. My eyes filled with tears as I recommitted my life to Jesus. As I made the decision, I felt the strength of the Lord surge through me, and His peace filled my heart and soul once again.

The next morning, I went to my father and told him of my decision. "Dad, I know that you love me and that you care for me. I just cannot leave Jesus and return to Islam, because He loves me more than anyone could possibly imagine. I am sorry that I cannot accept the offer that you have placed before me. Nevertheless, be assured that I still love you, and I have nothing against you. I just hope that you can understand the decision I have made." My father was furious. He threw a tantrum and expressed his anger in no uncertain terms. He called the elders of the mosque to a meeting at the house that morning.

When the elders came, they tried to convince me of the foolishness of my decision to follow Jesus and explained at length the struggles I would face in life. It was only by the strength and the grace of the Lord that I was able to face them and stand firm in my decision to follow the Lord. My father, in the presence of the elders of the mosque, and a few of my uncles wrote out a legal document disowning me and banishing me from his home and inheritance. The men from the mosque signed and sealed it. He gave me a copy and chucked me out of the house immediately. All this happened within a few hours, but throughout this episode, the grace of the Lord was with me, His wonderful presence engulfing me completely. From that day on, the Lord gave me renewed fervor to take His gospel to many people.

"Into His Vineyard"

Matthew 20:2

I completed three years at the Bible college, and the Lord helped me to graduate with excellence. I had gained great confidence in sharing the gospel with the unreached. My heart's desire was to share the love of Jesus with Muslims. I felt that the Lord had placed this special call upon my life to take the gospel to the Muslims. Whenever I saw Muslims on the roads, in the malls or shops, or in any other place, a great burden would fill my heart.

I adopted the traditional approach of distributing printed material to all the houses in a Muslim area and sharing the gospel with each person who opened the door. I took a few hundred tracts every day and knocked on doors. This went on for a few months. The task was not at all easy, and there were no positive responses. However, the burden for my people inside me never diminished. I knew that the ground would be hard, and it would take time before we would ever see the first results. After all, it took me two years after hearing the gospel for the first time from my teacher to start following Jesus. In addition to that, it took a miracle from the Lord in revealing Himself to me. I was not deterred by the initial lack of responses.

Making of a
Covenant

February 5, 1993, was an unforgettable day in my life. At the wedding of a mutual friend, I met Grace, who would become my wife some five years later. Though both of us attended the same church and had heard of each other, we had never met because of the large attendance at church. I had heard her unique story from some of her relatives who were my friends in the church.

Her father, who was a Hindu, accepted Jesus and started walking in His ways. But he died and went to be with the Lord when Grace was only eleven years of age. Her mother, who was angry that her husband passed away, reverted back to Hinduism. However, Grace and her siblings continued to trust in Jesus. They were persecuted by their mother, who beat them and even tore their Bibles, yet they persisted in following Jesus. Persecution did not deter Grace from believing in Jesus; she grew stronger in her faith and love for the Lord. The day we met, it was as if the Lord God connected our hearts together, and both of us knew immediately that we would spend the rest of our lives together.

The Lord did many things to show us that He loved us and performed many miracles in our lives. Our marriage was a miracle. Grace's mother, as a Hindu, did not want me to marry her daughter. She opposed us with all her heart. We did not want to go against her wishes, so we waited. In the meantime, I finished my bachelor of theology program, and Grace was able to finish her nursing studies. After five years of waiting, the Lord made Grace's mother favorably inclined toward our wedding. My family was opposed to this marriage, and none of my relatives attended our wedding. In fact, when my wife and I later went to my father's house to seek his blessing, he burst out from the house, wildly swinging a machete. My wife and I were horrified at this and prayed that God would touch him. Despite this conflict and the fact that our finances were limited, God provided in innumerable ways to give us a wonderful wedding beyond our expectations.

After our marriage, we settled in another town where I was already sharing the love of Jesus with Muslims. It was a struggle to make both ends meet since we did not have any kind of organizational backing. Some of the Christian leaders that I approached said, "Syed, we understand your burden for Muslims, but this is one area of ministry that doesn't yield much fruit. We need some kind of results to show to all our supporters. Therefore, you either change your focus group or seek support elsewhere." It was heartbreaking to see that some of the Christian leaders were very interested in hearing my story of coming to Jesus yet did not care to see similar things among other Muslims. They seemed to view it as nearly impossible to reach Muslims. However, the Lord took care of us in a wonderful manner. Though we started our life together with almost nothing, He made it clear that He was with us by taking care of every single need, and to this day, we have never lacked anything, just as the Word of God says,

> *The lions may grow weak and hungry, but those who seek the Lord lack no good thing.*—Psalm 34:10

"No Sorcery or Divination"

Numbers 23:23

In the year 2000, I was leading a church in a city as well as continuing to talk to Muslims about Jesus. It was at this time that my mother came to visit us after we had our first daughter. She wanted to spend time with her granddaughter. My mother was still a strong Muslim. She scolded me and openly expressed her anger at my leaving Islam. Even after these many years, her disgust and contempt of me never diminished.

Yet, amid all this, I continually talked to her about Jesus. I persistently invited her to the church that I was leading. She continually turned me down. My wife and I were undeterred and shared the love of Jesus with her at every available opportunity. Finally, because of our persistence, she agreed to come to church but said that she would be there for only a short time and that I should not introduce her to the church or even mention her name to any of the church members.

She arrived about half an hour late and sat in a chair at the farthest corner of the church, trying to appear as inconspicuous as possible. After a time of singing praises to God, I opened up the Bible and shared God's Word with the people. The Lord had given me a special message to preach that Sunday, which I distinctly remember. It was about the Lord's protection for the Israelites when they came out from Egypt. The Lord protected them with a pillar of fire. I spoke of many instances where the Lord used fire to vindicate His people, particularly from the story of Elijah. I explained that when God's people are in Christ, they enjoy a fortress of protection around them against all evil forces. I felt the Lord's presence and that He was working in the hearts of the people. I finally said, "If anyone here wants this kind of protection in your life, all you need is Jesus; He not only redeemed us from sin but also from all the powers of the evil one."

As I invited people to come speak with me about following Jesus, the first person to come toward me was my mother. I was flabbergasted. She knelt down at the front of the church with tears streaming down her cheeks. I could not believe my eyes. I thought that perhaps she had misunderstood some part of what I had said, so I bent down and said to her, "Mom, did you understand my question? I had asked only those people who wanted to follow Jesus to come to the front."

She said, "Yes, I understood perfectly. And yes, I want to follow Jesus." I rejoiced in my heart, and the entire church rejoiced with me when I announced that she was my mother. I joyfully led her in a prayer to accept Jesus as Lord.

After I reached home, I asked her, "Mom, what was that all about? Until this morning you were not even willing to hear about Jesus, let alone come to the church. We were surprised enough when you came to the church, but you surprised us even more when you came to the front of the church. Why have you suddenly made this decision? Tell us what happened." As my wife and I listened, she narrated to us the following incident.

It happened soon after I had made my decision to follow Christ. My uncles and aunts were intent on bringing me back into the fold of Islam. My mother was very irate and upset with me for following Jesus. She was aware that all the schemes of my relatives, family, and friends did not stop me from going to the church and reading my Bible. She also realized that though they beat me, I was not coming back to Islam, that nothing would deter me from following Jesus.

Therefore, she decided to take a drastic step to bring me back to Islam. She resorted to black magic. Many say that the black magic in Islam is one of the strongest kinds of witchcraft, much like the voodoo of Africa or Haiti.

My mother went to a woman who was very experienced in the art of black magic and explained the situation to her. She recounted that I had left Islam and become an infidel and that she wanted to bring me back to Islam at any cost. This woman listened intently and assured her it was not a difficult thing to do. The people who are involved in this type of work ask for a lock of hair or a piece of cloth belonging to the desired target of magic. My mother had come prepared with my clothing and a few of my hairs. After receiving the necessary things from my mother and the required money, along with a piece of paper on which my name was written, she locked herself in a room to perform the intended black magic.

After a while, the woman ran out of the room, returned everything to my mother, including the money and the paper on which my name was written, and said, "Please get out of here at once."

My mother was stunned and could see the woman was literally shaking from head to foot. My mother asked her, "What's the matter?" She refused to answer and just repeated her previous command but more firmly.

My mother insisted that she know what had happened. The woman explained, "As I performed the necessary magic, I saw that your son, Syed, was surrounded by a great wall of fire, more powerful than anything I have ever seen in all my life, and this wall of fire was shielding him. As I sent my powerful *jinn* (spirits) toward your son, they burned up. I have lost some of my powers today because of your son. The fire surrounding your son is very holy and very powerful. None of my *jinn* could even go near it. This kind of protection could only be from a God greater than the one I serve. It is better that you leave from here as soon as possible, because I am afraid that I will lose all my powers and have nothing to make my living from. Moreover, it is wiser to leave your son alone and not do anything against him. He has a great protection around him, and no power of any kind or any kind of magic can ever penetrate that protection."

My mother was astounded. She did not know how to react. She saw that the woman was still trembling and much disoriented. My mother kept thinking about this "wall of fire" for many years to come. I had no idea that all this had taken place. The opposition from my mother had lessened after a few years. Though she had stopped beating me, she continued using abusive language. I had even wondered why she had stopped beating me and what had caused a change in her behavior.

After committing her life to Jesus, she said, "I had been thinking about this 'wall of fire' for these many years. I still remember that the lady who did black magic was so terrified of that 'fire' that she was shaking and disoriented. The fire that she talked about had been bothering me for many years. I inquired of many people in a subtle manner, whether it was possible for any person to be surrounded by fire and not know it, but none of them could give me an answer. Today, as you were speaking about the fire, it was as if I could literally see the fire around every person seated in the church. I now understand that the fire was the protection you had through Jesus Christ. I, too, wanted this protection. That is the reason I have now committed my life to follow Jesus."

I was reminded of the Word of God,

> *There is no sorcery against Jacob, no divination against Israel. It will now be said of Jacob and of Israel, "See what God has done!"*—Numbers 23:23

We were filled with joy that God showed Himself mighty and that He works in ways that we cannot see or comprehend. His ways are higher than ours, and His purposes are loftier than our noblest intentions. When the Lord allows us to go through certain circumstances, we might not be able to see it, but He is there, working out His perfect will for the glory of His matchless name and for the extension of His divine kingdom. I had the honor of baptizing my mother in the same church a month later. She is now a strong follower of Jesus and an active member in her church.

God is always with those who love Him. He has a wonderful purpose and plan behind all of our needs and diseases, our afflictions and persecutions, our heartaches and tears. God is in control of every situation. His Word says,

> *And we know that in all things God works for the good of those who love him, who have been called according to His purpose.*—Romans 8:28

"As for Me and My Household"

Joshua 24:15

In 2004 the Lord told me, in a dream, to go meet my father once again. By this time, he had remarried and moved on to another city. I reached his house with my wife and daughter. He did not let us in, and we stood outside for a long time, waiting for him to open the door. He was still very angry with me for forsaking Islam. My stepmother eventually opened the door for us. Though my father's countenance softened a little when he saw our daughter, he did not say a word during our visit.

Over the next few years, I continued to visit my father regularly; the Lord started to chip away at his hardheartedness, and we were eventually able to have a conversation. However, when I talked about Jesus, he became furious. Slowly, the Lord has worked in his heart, and though my dad has not yet acknowledged Jesus, he will listen to what I have to say about Jesus. I am reminded of the Christian brother who had said that I would never be able to share the truth with my dad if I did not accept his offer. But God changed the whole situation with my dad, and our relationship has grown stronger over the years. We call each other often, and he now shows interest in our lives. The Lord has been restoring not only our relationship but also our love for each other. As the years went by, my dad lost all of his wealth due to some bad investments and his second wife's extravagance. He divorced his second wife, sold all he had to pay off his debts, and is currently living with extended family in our native village.

Recently, the Lord gave us an amazing opportunity. He gave me a great love and burden in my heart for my people—my paternal uncles, aunts, cousins, and other relatives who were angry with me for forsaking Islam. It had been nearly twenty-four years since I had seen any of them. They had not met my wife or my children. For many months, the Lord had been speaking to me of the need for sharing the good news of Jesus with my extended family. I talked with my dad about it, and he was not very pleased with the idea. He was afraid that some kind of harm might befall me at the hands of my relatives and doubtful as to whether my family members would even want to meet with me. He cautioned me that I might not be welcome in their homes. It did not matter to me whether I would be welcomed or not, my desire was to share the good news of Jesus with them. This might be the only opportunity for them to hear this news, and I knew the Lord wanted me to share with them.

As my wife, my three children, and I made the trip to the village of my relatives, some 150 kilometers from my city, I had knots in my stomach. I did not know what awaited us, but the loving and comforting presence of our Lord Jesus gave me a deep sense of peace. I had told my dad to inform all of them that we were coming to visit them. However, he had chosen not to inform them because of his concern for our safety. Nevertheless, we visited our relatives one by one. My dad came along with us for the visits.

The same people who had persecuted me, tortured me, starved me, beaten me, and even tried to kill me now welcomed me in their homes. Although we had surprised them with our visit, we were able to meet with most of them, and above all, the Lord helped me to share with all of them about the love of Jesus. A few were not happy with what I was telling them. Some even started arguing, but there was no hatred in their arguments. I was able to share my testimony, and people were surprised to hear how God had cared for us. With my dad beside me, I said, "My earthly father sent me out of his house and disowned me, but my heavenly Father has never forsaken us and is still taking care of us wonderfully." This was a very powerful statement because many of my uncles were present when my father wrote out the legal document disowning me. All my relatives knew that my dad had lost everything and was now dependent on us.

I could see that God was turning their hearts favorably toward the good news of Jesus. I shared with them how, on the cross, Jesus had not only taken away my sins but also my shame and guilt. Almost all of them sat and listened as I pointed out various passages about Jesus, from both the Qur'an and the *Injil* (the Bible). I asked each of them why Allah would make *Isa al Masih* (Jesus Christ) so special. Why would Allah give Jesus special titles like *Kalimatullah* (Word of Allah), *Ruhullah* (Spirit of Allah) and *Al-Masih* (the Christ). I also asked them why only Jesus was sinless and not any of the other prophets. None of them could answer. I also spoke to them about the various miracles, parables, and sayings of Jesus, both from the Qur'an and from the *Injil*.

Please join with us in praying for my dad and all my relatives who have heard about Jesus yet don't believe. Kindly pray that the Lord will open up their eyes and hearts so they will be able to see Jesus, just as John the Baptist says,

> *Behold, the Lamb of God, who takes away*
> *the sins of the world!*—John 1:29

Continuing the
Journey
with Christ

When I think of the Lord's care and the blessings He has graciously bestowed, especially the blessing of knowing Jesus, the one who took away our sin and shame through His great victory on the cross, I am passionate to share Jesus with everyone. The Lord has given me a great burden for my beloved Muslim people such that I would gladly go and share the good news of Jesus anywhere in the world. Indeed, the Lord has asked us to go to a restricted country to share about Christ with Muslims. Our hearts desire and prayer is that all Muslims around the world would have eternal life just as is written in God's Word.

Now this is eternal life: that they may know you, the only true God, and Jesus Christ, whom you have sent.—John 17:3

For a quarter of a century, the Lord has been leading me in my walk with Him and in His work. Though it has been a long and difficult journey sharing with Muslims, the Lord has been gracious in supplying the required strength. My wife and children have been appreciative and supportive in all our ventures, and we look forward to reaching out in innovative ways to many more Muslims in the years to come.

As I look back on my journey with Christ, I am filled with awe, gratitude, and praise for our loving Lord Jesus, who has never failed, not in His love and forgiveness nor in His patience and faithfulness. The words, "Try me, I am Jesus" not only changed my life on this earth but also for eternity. *"Glory be to Him who turns the hearts of men."*

Printed in the United States
By Bookmasters